BIOGRAPHIES FOR KIDS ALL ABOUT PRINCESS DIANA

LEARNING ABOUT ALL HER HUMANITARIAN EFFORTS

CHILDREN'S BIOGRAPHIES OF FAMOUS PEOPLE BOOKS

BABY PROFESSOR

EDUCATION KIDS

Speedy Publishing LLC
40 E. Main St. #1156
Newark, DE 19711
www.speedypublishing.com

Who is the beloved
Princess of Wales?
Let's read about the
beautiful Princess Diana!

On July 1, 1961, near
Sandringham, England,
Princes Diana was born to
Edward John Spencer and
Frances Ruth Burke Roche.

Unfortunately, her parents got divorced while she was young. Her father was given custody of her and her siblings.

IAM III

She studied at Riddlesworth Hall and later on transferred to West Heath School.

She was known to be shy
but she showed interest
in dancing and in music.
She exhibited a great
fondness for children.

She moved to London
after graduating from the
Institut Alpin Videmanette.
Eventually, she became a
kindergarten teacher at
the Young England School.

On July 29, 1981, Princess Diana got married to the heir of the British throne, Prince Charles.

They were blessed with two sons namely, Prince William Arthur Philip Louis and Prince Henry Charles Albert David also known as Prince Harry.

The couple got
divorced in 1996.

LK·THE DIANA·PRINCE

OF WALES MEMORIAL

On August 30, 1997, while
she was trying to escape
the paparazzi in Paris,
she got involved in a car
accident and died.

Princess Diana was one of the most admired members of the British royal family.

THE DIANA PRINCESS

WALES MEMORIAL

She was very generous and helpful. She was a strong supporter of many charity works, especially those that targeted children.

She worked with the
homeless, the needy and
the poorest of the poor.
She helped and rendered
selfless service for HIV
and AIDS victims.

She devoted her time
to helping others and to
her sons. She organized
missions and built hospitals
that specialized in the
treatment of cancer like,
Royal Marsden Hospital
and Great Ormond Street
Hospital for Sick Children.

She also led an organization for the homeless - The National Arts Trust and The Leprosy Mission.

Princess Diana also became a Patron of the English National Ballet, which highlighted her passion for arts. In her lifetime, she was noted to have been a patron of more than 100 charities.

She became the President of
Barnardo's, a British charity
that helps the children to
reach their dreams and
show their potentials.

Today, Princess Diana is remembered as true humanitarian. She is admired by everyone. Her warmth and genuine concern for the situation of the people can never be forgotten.

Did you like the story of
Princess Diana? Share
it with your friends!

Visit
BABY PROFESSOR
EDUCATION KIDS
www.BabyProfessorBooks.com
to download Free Baby Professor eBooks
and view our catalog of new and exciting
Children's Books